Miracles In The Making

I am very proud to have played a small part in the events so ably described in this book. I found reading *Miracles in the Making* to be stimulating, thought-provoking—yes, even *exciting* reading. And for those who have not yet utilized the miracle of healing prayer—try it. You will surely believe.

Robert Young
star of *Father Knows Best*
& *Marcus Welby, M.D.*

The author (center) with Olga and Ambrose Worrall.

Miracles In The Making

Scientific Evidence for the Effectiveness of Prayer

by Robert N. Miller, Ph.D.

ARIEL PRESS
Atlanta, Georgia

Many of the experimental results in this book have already been presented in various scientific papers and journals. These include:

Chapter 7—first appeared in a 1967 issue of *The Journal of Pastoral Counseling.*

Chapter 8—first appeared in the July 1974 issue of *Science of Mind* magazine.

Chapter 9—first appeared in *Human Dimensions,* Vol. 5, No. 1 & 2, pp. 22-26, 1976.

Chapter 10—first appeared in the international medical journal, *Medical Hypotheses,* Vol. 8, pp. 481-490, 1982.

ISBN 0-89804-096-5

Dedication

This book is dedicated to my wife, Genevieve Miller, and to Olga Worrall, first lady of spiritual healing.

Genevieve, my beloved helpmate and lifelong inspiration, encouraged me to continue to seek help for our retarded twins after doctors told us there was nothing they could do to aid their mental development. Once we had discovered the unique healing gifts of Ambrose and Olga Worrall, she assisted me in planning and conducting the experiments which demonstrate the reality of healing energies.

Genevieve helped me prepare the talks that I presented at conferences on healing. She accompanied Olga and me to give an invited paper at King's College at the University of London, as well as to Lourdes, where we investigated the properties of the water at the shrine where Bernadette first saw her vision of Mary. Without Genevieve's encouragement, patience, and support, the research reported in this book would not have been possible.

Olga Worrall opened a whole new dimension

in our lives and thinking. The evening I first met her, she asked me, "Has your mother passed away? There is someone standing beside you who says she is your mother." Olga then described my mother in great detail, down to the opal ring she used to wear on her finger. My mother had been dead for twenty years.

Olga then communicated information from my mother. It was like having a three-way telephone conversation. My mother mentioned incidents that occurred after she passed on. I began to realize that she had been actively following the life of the family since she died—and that she was actually present in the room speaking to me—through Olga. She was invisible, but just as "real" as ever.

That evening, as I drove back to my hotel, I felt as if I were flying. I knew that, beyond all doubt, my mother was alive. Life after death is a reality, not a theological concept.

Genevieve and I became good friends with Olga and her husband Ambrose and learned much about life from them. Perhaps the most important thing we learned was that prayer is effective. We can ask for and receive help as we need it!

Olga was always available to us, with cheer and practical advice. Through the years, Olga was instrumental in healing thousands of individuals who came to her with their problems. She also shared her knowledge and talents by lecturing—and by participating in scientific tests.

In recognition of her unique gifts and unselfish contributions to the advancement of healing knowledge, she was awarded a doctor of philosophy degree by the Church of Religious Science, and was also honored as a doctor of humane letters.

In a newsletter announcing Olga's passing, author Harold Sherman wrote: "When I think of Olga, I think of the beauty of a sunset. The sun is soon gone, but the afterglow remains. Her afterglow will linger and abide with us forever and a day."

Contents

Foreword

This book includes the results of a five-year study on the mechanism of effective prayer sponsored by the Holmes Center for Research in Holistic Healing. The author is grateful to Dr. Willis Kinnear for his vision in seeing the need for and in organizing the Holmes Research Center.

Special thanks are due to Ambrose and Olga Worrall for so generously contributing their time and unique talents in conducting many of the scientific experiments reported herein.

Other healers who participated in this program were Dr. William Miller, Reverend Robert Love, Reverend Dorothy Love, Reverend Alex Holmes, Dr. Vetura Papke, Mr. Benjamin Bibb and Reverend Richard Batzler. Dr. Neal Schulman and Dr. Joseph Hertell helped design the statistical study on the effectiveness of remote mental healing. Linda Lee was indispensable in organizing and recording data and in analyzing the results of the statistical study. Dr. Edward Brame, a senior scientist with the Du Pont Company and an international authority on the subject of infrared spectroscopy, conducted the analyses of energized water. The enthusiasm and wholehearted cooperation of each of these individuals were major factors in the success of this project.

Grateful acknowledgement is also made to Robert Young, Gloria Swanson, Dr. Ballentine Henley, Asa Bushnell, and all the other contributors to the Holmes Research Center. Without their support the research programs described in this monograph would not have been undertaken.

The research studies on healing and healing energies which are described in this book have all been previously published in various journals. Because there is renewed interest in the subject of healing and healing energies, it was felt that compiling these studies into one book would make the information more available, not only to those who are seeking health and healing, but also to doctors and nurses using healing energies in one form or another in their daily work and to scientists who are interested in conducting additional research on healing energies.

Each experimental section was originally written to conform to the style of the journal or magazine in which it was published. For example, *Medi-*

cal Hypotheses, the medical journal which published the "Study on the Effectiveness of Remote Mental Healing," required that the paper be written in the third person and include a review of the literature and full experimental details. This enables other investigators to duplicate the experiments and use the techniques for further research.

It is hoped that the information in this book will help those who want to improve their health or other conditions in their life, will encourage members of the medical profession to use the principles of healing in their daily work, and will inspire scientists and other investigators to do additional work on the subject of effective prayer and healing energies.

—Dr. Robert N. Miller

Miracles In The Making

1

In Need of a Miracle

The question of why some prayers are answered and many are not has puzzled mankind for hundreds of years. The Bible and more recent literature are filled with accounts of prayers being answered in miraculous ways. Until the nineteenth century the accepted explanation for miraculous answers to prayers was that God heard the pleas and responded in ways which seemed to disregard universal physical laws and forces. The parting of the Red Sea when the Israelites fled Egypt is a prime example of such an occurrence.

In the the latter part of the nineteenth century, ministers and scientists who studied the subject of healing and answers to prayer began to record certain patterns and phenomena which seemed to be related to successful healing events. Among other things, they discovered that, although God supplies the forces and energies needed for successful healings, humans frequently facilitate

God's designs by acting as His agents on earth.

My wife Genevieve and I became intensely interested in the subject of prayer and healing in 1956 when our twins, Bobbie and Kristie, were born. At that time I was teaching chemical engineering at the Georgia Institute of Technology and Genevieve was singing in the Atlanta Symphony Orchestra Chorus under the direction of Robert Shaw.

During their first year, we noticed that Bobbie and Kristie were slow to develop verbal and motor skills, and had them examined by a psychologist. After analyzing the results of many tests, he informed us that they were severely retarded and the medical profession could do nothing to accelerate their mental development. He suggested that our best course might be to put them in an institution.

Genevieve and I were devastated by this news. It was a rock bottom moment in our lives. We saw the psychologist in the morning, then had lunch at the Purple Cow restaurant in Buckhead in north Atlanta. Despite our anguish, we did manage some smiles when we read the menu with its outrageous Purple Cow limericks describing the food offerings.

Although we were floored by the news, we refused to accept the psychologist's recommendation. During the next year, we painstakingly followed up all possible avenues of help.

We also prayed a great deal.

When I was a child, I said my prayers every night before I went to bed. As I grew older, however, I prayed only when I had a serious problem. I prayed not because I believed my prayers would be answered, but because I had tried all other possible solutions to my problem and finally turned to prayer just in case there was something to it.

In church and Sunday school I learned of the many people who were healed by Jesus. Here, apparently, was a man whose prayers were answered immediately. However, I figured that it happened only for Jesus some two thousand years ago—and certainly could not happen today. I often wondered if the accounts were true or if they had been exaggerated by the scribes of the day.

Little did I suspect, as a young man, how important the miracle healings which are described in the Bible were to become in my life—or how much relevance these events of two thousand years ago can have on modern living!

Take, for example, the story of the healing that occurred in a synagogue. A woman had been crippled for eighteen years. She was bent double and unable to stand upright. When Jesus saw her He called to her and said, "You are rid of your problem." Then He laid his hands on her and, at once, she straightened up and began to praise God.

From my perspective, the key seems to be that the woman was healed when Jesus touched her. He didn't ask her if she had faith. He didn't tell her that her sins were forgiven. He simply placed his hands on her and she was well.

Then there is the case of the woman who was healed of hemorraging by touching the hem of Jesus's garment. She came to a gathering of Jesus and His followers believing that she would be healed if she could only touch his robe. She attained her objective and was healed. However, at the instant she touched his robe, Jesus felt the virtue—the healing energy of God—flowing from him.

Looking at this case objectively, there was direct contact with a source of healing power and a strong measure of faith element.

A third example is that of the nobleman's son who was sick to the point of death at Capernaum. The nobleman asked Jesus to heal his son. Instead of going to the nobleman's home, Jesus said, "Your son will live." The father believed and, upon his return to his home, found that the fever had left his son when Jesus had said, "Your son will live."

This case differs from the others. There was no direct contact between the healer and the patient, no expression of faith on the part of the patient—although the father strongly believed—and the healing occurred miles from the young man's sickbed.

These are truly miraculous healings. The least we can say is that they occurred in a mysterious manner. However, we must remember that all scientific laws and energies were mysterious to us before science discovered their underlying principles.

When I was in college and learned about atoms, electrons, quantum mechanics, and physics, I became convinced that everything happens according to law. If an event cannot be explained by known laws or principles, it was either inaccurately reported or we do not yet know the scientific laws which are applicable. The many cases of how science explained the reasons for old superstitions by uncovering the nugget of truth behind them led me to believe there had to be a scientific reason for anything that happens in the universe.

Meanwhile, I continued to go to church and pray with the rest of the congregation, just in case. I wanted to believe what I heard from the pulpit on Sunday, but my logical mind would not accept the validity of the Biblical stories of prayers being answered in miraculous ways.

This odd mixture of interest and doubt was my state of mind regarding prayer when we became aware of the problems our twins were facing.

2

Looking At Alternatives

Realizing we could expect little or no help for our twins from the medical profession, Genevieve and I began to seriously investigate the subject of miracle healings and the effects of prayer.

We learned that miraculous healings occurred before the time of Christ. They took place in ancient Egypt during the reign of the Pharaoh of the Third Dynasty. Imhotep, the famous sage and physician of that era, was associated with some of these healings.

They also occurred during the time period described by the Old Testament. Elisha cured Naaman of leprosy by telling him to bathe in the River Jordon seven times. When Naaman did this, he was healed. The approximate time of this occurrence was 894 B.C. This information helped explode one of my misconceptions—that the miracle healings were associated only with Jesus.

In my readings I came across frequent references to a mysterious energy which seems to be related to healing and the mechanism through which prayers are answered. The Chinese claim that man is filled with *chi,* a vital energy or life force. The universe too, they say, is charged with this vital energy and, under the proper conditions, man can draw upon an inexhaustible supply.

In India, the Hindus speak of a similar energy which is present in the body and in the universe. They call it *prana,* or "the essence of life." Yoga teaches and emphasizes breathing exercises whereby prana can be drawn into the body to restore its depleted energies.

A man who did a most comprehensive and scientific investigation of this remarkable energy was Karl von Reichenbach, who was born in the kingdom of Wurtemberg in 1768 and died in 1869. He called it the *odic* force because, like the power of Odin in ancient Norse mythology, it permeates everything in heaven and earth.

Reichenbach was a brilliant chemist and had a Ph. D. degree in science. He was the discoverer of both creosote and paraffin. His researches into magnetism led him to a discovery which, perhaps, he never would have made had he not had the help of sensitives, persons with a much wider range of sensory response than the average human being. These individuals were supersensitive to hot and cold and could see high frequency light waves which are invisible to most people.

Reichenbach found that when sensitives looked at a magnet in a dark room they could see emanations which they described as streams of light. They could see similar emanations from certain metals, from crystals, from matter which was undergoing chemical changes, and from the human body. The visible radiations from humans were much more marked in some people but visible in all.

Karl von Reichenbach found that these supersensitive people experienced a disagreeable feeling when someone shook hands with them in a normal manner, right hand grasping right hand. However, if someone grasped both their hands, right hand to left and left hand to right, a warm and comfortable sensation was produced. This indicates that all human beings generate this energy and that it has polarity, just like magnetic energy. In fact, modern investigators do refer to it as biomagnetic energy. This odic force or biomagnetic energy in humans is increased by taking food, by being in the sunshine, and by general physical fitness.

In his writings, Reichenbach tells us that odic force is discharged through the fingertips. It is retained for some time in matter charged by it and is retained longest in oil. It is an interesting fact that the oil used in the healing services of the early church was blessed by being held in a bishop's hand.

About fifty years ago, Dr. Leslie Weatherhead, the famous English theologian, became greatly interested in Reichenbach's work. Dr. Weatherhead said, "One might call odic force the all-pervading energy. It was discovered or rediscovered a hundred years ago, though its discoverer was scorned, derided, insulted, and then ignored. At the present time inquiry into it is leading us into a conception of a part of the universe as epoch-making and wonderful as astronomy has made the starry heavens, and as nuclear physics has made atomic energy."

Dr. Weatherhead proved to himself that this odic force or biomagnetic energy is related to healing. He had been observing some scientific experiments with a Dr. Ash of Harley Street in London. Dr. Ash seemed to have an unusual amount of this vital energy and could heal people of a wide variety of ailments by merely pointing his fingers at the area which was afflicted. Here are Dr. Weatherhead's own words which describe his observations and his explanations for what happened:

"Where there is pain in the body, psychic energy is being lost, much as static electricity is lost by running to earth. At this 'pain-point,' by holding his hands in a certain position almost touching the skin, Dr. Ash appears able to drive his own odic force into a body, powerfully enough to send it up the nerve paths to the cause of the pain, often with what appear to be miraculously therapeutic results. This is what Mrs. Salmon does, though she calls it the power of Christ, and what Mr. Edwards does. [Mrs. Salmon and Mr. Edwards were two famous English healers.] Dr. Ash believes it to be a perfectly normal form of energy not yet understood, but rapidly coming under the survey and understanding of science."

On one occasion, Dr. Weatherhead was invited by Dr. Ash to try to determine which part of a patient's back was causing her distress, as she lay face downward on a couch with her back exposed. When Dr. Weatherhead ran his hands down her back, about one inch from the skin surface, he felt a sensation of pins and needles in his hand at one particular point of the spine. This turned out to be the focal point of the pain. Dr. Ash said the emanations from the pain-point interacting with the odic force from Dr. Weatherhead's hand produced the prickly sensation in his fingertips.

On another occasion Dr. Ash was treating a

little three-year-old girl who had been discharged from a famous children's hospital in London, her mother having been told that the child had been injured at birth and would never walk. Again, in Dr. Weatherhead's own words:

"I held my own hands with Dr. Ash's in the appropriate place at the base of the spine, and our delight can be imagined when the child moved her limbs for the first time in her life and said, 'Mummy, I can move my legs.' Her mother was overcome with tears of joy and, indeed, we were all deeply moved."

Apparently, then, this odic force or biomagnetic energy flows from the hands of certain gifted individuals and, in certain instances, can bring about dramatic healings.

In 1937, about seventy-five years after Reichenbach did his research on the odic force, Drs. Glasser and Barth of the department of biophysics of the Cleveland Clinic reported on a significant research project which helps provide a scientific basis for the existence of a biomagnetic energy. They were investigating 'mitogenetic radiation,' which is merely a new name for the odic force of Reichenbach. They had become aware of the energy or radiation which was emitted by plants—and also as the result of chemical reactions—and worked with both physical and biological detectors in attempting to quantitatively measure this energy. Their biological detectors were day-old cultures of yeast in quartz tubes. These were exposed to various sources of mitogenetic radiation and the increase in the number of yeast cells after overnight incubation was then related to the amount of energy absorbed. Their standard method of generating the energy was to mix solutions of ferrosulphate and potassium dichromate.

In later experiments Dr. Glasser and Dr. Barth developed high sensitivity Geiger-Muller tubes which could detect this subtle form of energy. This, to my knowledge, was the first instance of recording this mysterious energy on a scientific instrument.

Then, in 1965 Dr. Bernard Grad of the department of physiology, University of Manitoba, confirmed the concept that the energy from the hands of certain individuals has healing properties. In his paper, "The Biological Effects of the Laying On of Hands," he describes a scientifically rigorous experiment in which forty-eight female mice were divided into two groups.

A wound was made on the back of each mouse by cutting away a circle of skin approximately one-half inch in diameter. The area of each wound was accurately measured by tracing the outline on a piece of paper.

One group of mice was treated by a man who had demonstrated healing ability, a Colonel Estebany who was a retired Hungarian army officer. He placed the treatment cage between his hands, the cage resting in his left palm, and held his right hand just over the wire mesh covering the animals. He treated the animals in this way fifteen minutes each time, twice daily, five days a week. The control group of mice, also in a cage, were picked up in the same manner but were not exposed to the hand treatment.

At the end of fourteen days the wound areas on the mice which were exposed to the healer's hands were healing twice as fast as the mice who were not treated! These results clearly indicate that, during the treatment periods, some form of healing energy flowed from Colonel Estebany's hands to the mice.

So, with each new scientific contribution, the exploration of this elusive healing force is emerging from the area of folk lore to a modern study on the frontiers of science. It is also becoming increasingly clear that the mysterious properties of prayer and healing can be revealed by scientific method.

My personal experience with this energy began in 1965, when I first met Ambrose and Olga Worrall.

3

We Meet The Worralls

One day, I read in *Reader's Digest* about an aircraft engineer in Baltimore who successfully healed people with serious ailments by placing his hands on them and praying for them. His name was Ambrose Worrall.

A few weeks later, in my capacity as staff scientist for Lockheed Aircraft Corporation, I flew to Washington on a business trip. I called Mr. Worrall's home in the hope that I could drive to Baltimore and meet with him. His wife, Olga, answered the telephone. She told me that Ambrose was out of town but that she would be glad to see me.

Olga was a pleasant, motherly woman about five feet six inches tall and in her sixties. My visit with her proved to be one of the most fascinating evenings of my life.

I learned that Olga was born in Cleveland, Ohio on November 30, 1906 to a Russian theologian father and a Roman Catholic mother, a Hungarian countess. From the age of three, Olga had the ability to heal individuals by just touching them. She graduated from Cleveland West Commerce High School and from Cleveland Business University. After coming to Baltimore, she taught business and mathematics courses at Eastern High School before retiring from teaching in the mid-1950's.

After she met Ambrose, her husband-to-be, she discovered that, in addition to being an engineer and aerospace consultant he, too, was a healer. Ambrose conducted countless private healing sessions in their home, with Olga assisting. Olga opened the New Life Clinic in the Mt. Washington Methodist Church in Baltimore and maintained weekly healing sessions for 28 years. Neither Olga nor Ambrose ever accepted any payment, love offering, or gifts of any kind throughout their long years of healing service. They each felt that their God-given healing talents were to be shared freely with all who asked for them.

Olga showed me a stack of letters written by individuals who had been healed of a variety of ailments, as well as from doctors whose patients had been helped by treatments from Olga and Ambrose.

I told Olga of our twins' problems. She said that she and her husband would pray for them and that we should bring them to Baltimore for a laying-on-of-hands treatment. We took Bobbie and Kristie to the Worralls for numerous treatments. They improved mentally and physically far beyond the doctor's expectations. They learned to read and write and Kristie was actually able to do simple algebra problems.

Were these miracles? Genevieve and I thought so. How did they occur? I was determined to find out.

Bobbie & Kristie Miller with Olga and Ambrose.

4

We Witness Miracles

In addition to taking our twins to Baltimore to receive laying-on-of-hands and prayer treatments from the Worralls, we also took them to the healing services conducted by the New Life Clinic of the Mt. Washington Methodist Church in Baltimore.

Every Thursday morning at ten o'clock a prayer and healing service was—and still is—conducted. Essentially, it was an abbreviated church service. During the first hour, Olga would give a short talk related to healing and prayer. This was followed by a twenty-minute period of silent prayer and meditation.

The healing service would then begin with a prayer by the pastor of Mt. Washington Methodist Church. A hymn would be sung and the minister would preach a short sermon. Then, while the organ softly played, every member of the audience would come to the front to receive a laying-on-of-hands and prayers for healing from Olga or one of her ministerial assistants.

Through the years many healings occurred. A young girl, Gail Washington, suffered severe brain damage at birth and, by the time she was four, was deaf, blind and had a serious heart condition. She also stopped growing. Gail's mother consulted a brain specialist in New York. He told her that medicine could do no more for her daughter but suggested that she take Gail to one of Olga Worrall's healing services.

Gail's mother took her to the New Life Clinic many times over a period of several years. Gail's condition gradually improved, and she is now a bright, attractive young woman with good hearing and almost perfect eyesight.

Another youngster, Jeffrey Kenney, developed a crippling bone disease which, doctors said, would disable him for life. His mother, Mrs. James Kenney said, "I couldn't accept that, and Jeffrey couldn't accept it, either. He wanted so much to run and play like other boys. I took him to Mrs. Worrall's services. She not only prayed with us but also gave us faith that Jeffrey's leg could be cured—and it was."

A few years later Jeffrey was running and playing with other boys. The specially constructed leg brace that he previously had to wear was discarded. His doctor said, "Recovery did occur where, medically, it could not logically have been expected to happen."

A middle-aged Pennsylvania widow came to the New Life Clinic with a tumor the size of an egg in her cheek. Her doctor had sent her because of the danger that paralysis would result if he operated.

There was no sudden reaction when Olga placed her hands on her and prayed for her but, when the woman returned to her pew she exclaimed, "It's going! It's shrinking! It's healing!" The tumor had indeed gone down and eventually it disappeared.

The woman's physician stated, "I saw the tumor before the patient went to Baltimore and I saw it gone after she came home. Someone or something took it out, that's for sure."

5

Tapping the Unseen

Olga Worrall was not just an extraordinary healer, however; she had the ability to tap the unseen forces of life in other ways as well.

In the spring of 1979, Genevieve and I were building a new home thirty miles north of Atlanta. Olga came to Atlanta for a visit and, while we were discussing the new house, I asked her if she could help me locate the best spot for our well. She looked over the plat of the property and said, "Get me a pair of pliers."

Opening the pliers, she grasped one handle in each hand and rotated her hands inward until the jaws of the pliers pointed upward. Then, as she moved her hands over the plat, a powerful force seemed to pull the pliers downward until the jaws actually touched the paper.

Olga said, "You have a shale mound beneath the earth, but if you drill a well at that spot you will find water."

Sure enough, the well driller encountered a solid shale formation at 10 feet and, at 200 feet, struck a vein of water which gave a flow of five gallons a minute—more than adequate for normal household needs.

Several months later, we accompanied Olga on a visit to Honolulu, Hawaii. Olga was there to give a talk at a holistic healing seminar, and Genevieve and I were visiting our friend David Larsen, who manages agricultural projects in Hawaii and Malaysia.

We were in David's office discussing some of Olga's unique healings when she noticed that Kathy, David's secretary, had her right arm in a sling. Olga asked how it was injured. Kathy told us that in a karate class she had strained a ligament as she sparred with an opponent in practice. Olga placed her hands on the injured area for several minutes, then said, "Maybe that will help."

A little later, David asked Olga if she would help him find water on one of his plantations in Malaysia. Olga replied, "I'm not a dowser; I'm a healer."

"You helped Bob find water for his new home, didn't you?"

"Yes," said Olga, "but I had a plat to work from."

After David explained that a plat is simply a

map of a piece of property, Olga said, "I'm willing to try. Show me a map."

A few minutes later she was sitting at a table, a map of the Malayan plantation in front of her and a pencil in her right hand. With her eyes closed, she permitted her hand to wander over the map. Finally she put her pencil down at a precise point and said, "There is water here."

Through a magnifying glass, David looked at the mark she had made on the map. He said, "This won't do. You're in the middle of a river."

Olga laughed and said, "You wanted water didn't you?" She then repeated the procedure and marked two points on dry land.

David carefully put the map away and said he would send it to his assistant in Malaysia.

A few weeks later, after Olga had returned home to Baltimore, she received a letter dated June 24, 1979, from David Larsen.

"Dear Olga: You will be happy (but not surprised) to know that Kathy's arm started to improve within a few hours after you treated her. The next day she could use her hand and then the sling came off. She is very grateful—as I am....The enclosed map of Malaysia shows where you started your new career of water dowsing. I will let you know what happens ...."

The climax to this sequence of events came when Olga received a second letter from David dated December 12, 1979:

"Congratulations! Our manager from Malaysia was in the office this morning and he pointed out the locations of the two wells drilled on the plantation. These are the first wells ever drilled in this area, as there was not supposed to be any underground water. Both wells produce over *one million* gallons of water per day!"

6

Proving the Miracle

Through Olga, Genevieve and I met Dr. Willis Kinnear, the editor of *Science of Mind* magazine. Dr. Kinnear was also a member of the board of directors of the Ernest Holmes Research Foundation, which was sponsored and supported by the Church of Religious Science in Los Angeles.

The Church of Religious Science was founded fifty years ago by Ernest Holmes, a philosopher and profound thinker. Ernest Holmes was not satisfied with all of the teachings and practices of the "mainstream" church. He began to investigate Eastern religions and found that, although they were similar to Christianity in moral principles they, too, had many ceremonies and customs which his logical mind could not accept.

Ernest Holmes then extracted what he considered to be the essence of truth from all the religions. The result was the Science of Mind philosophy, which is advocated by the Church of Religious Science. Essentially, it teaches that man can control his own destiny through the proper use of his creative abilities. Through the use of a prayer procedure known as the Spiritual Mind Treatment, man can bring desirable conditions into his life.

The essential steps involved in the Spiritual Mind Treatment are:

(a) relaxation,

(b) attunement with a Higher Power,

(c) a visualization and affirmation of the situation desired, and

(d) an expression of thanks.

Inasmuch as one of the basic concepts of the Science of Mind philosophy is the healing of people and situations through prayer, the purpose of the Ernest Holmes Research Foundation was to sponsor and encourage research in the field of spiritual healing. The work of the Holmes Foundation was supported by the Church of Religious Science, which has its headquarters in Hollywood.

One of the staunch supporters of the foundation was Robert Young, who played Dr. Marcus Welby on the television series, and his wife, Betty. Robert Young told me that, before he joined the Church of Religious Science, he used to have severe headaches caused by the stresses of his acting career. After he began to apply the principles he learned from the Ernest Holmes teachings, his headaches disappeared and his life was vastly improved.

Gloria Swanson, the famous movie actress, was another well-known member of the Church of Religious Science. In addition to faithfully following the Science of Mind teachings, Gloria watched her diet very carefully and brought her own salads and fresh vegetables in a paper bag when she attended luncheons.

Robert Young, Gloria Swanson and Asa Bushnell, the binocular mogul, were especially generous in their support of the Ernest Holmes Research Foundation.

I was one of the first investigators to have his research sponsored by the Holmes Center. My assignment was to determine in the laboratory whether or not there is any validity to the theory that individuals can heal the sick, in their presence or at a distance, through the Spiritual Mind Treatment prayer procedure.

My project plan was based on the assumption that, if healing of physical ailments does occur as the result of laying-on-of-hands and spiritual mind treatments, there must be an energy involved. Therefore, the first task was to discover methods for detecting and measuring this energy.

The first year of the project was devoted to discovering methods for detecting the energies involved in healing. It was discovered that standard laboratory instruments such as thermometers, thermocouples, radiometers, and light meters are not affected. However, a biological detector, rye grass, provided dramatic evidence of the effect of thought energy on the growth rate of plants.

During the second year a cloud chamber was successfully used to register the effect of energy from a healer's hands. Subsequent experiments demonstrated that this energy will change the electrical characteristics of plants, will alter the color of copper salts crystallizing from aqueous solutions, and will change the surface tension and hydrogen bonding of water.

The project concluded with a statistical study on the effectiveness of remote mental healing. The details of these experiments are described in the following chapters.

Robert Young, Gloria Swanson, and Dr. Robert N. Miller take part in a healing symposium sponsored by the Church of Religious Science. Robert Young was moderator and master of ceremonies of the meeting.

7

Stimulating the Growth of Plants with Thoughts Alone

In his book, *The Power of Prayer on Plants*, Franklin Loehr describes experiments in which the growth rate of plants was accelerated as much as twenty percent when individuals, or groups of people, prayed for the plants in a systematic, disciplined manner. The recommended method of praying was to visualize the plant thriving under ideal conditions. The growth rate of the plants was determined by measuring their height with a ruler at relatively long intervals ranging from several days to several weeks.

In 1936 Dr. H. Kleuter of the United States Department of Agriculture developed a very accurate and effective method of measuring plant growth by using a rotary electrical transducer connected to a strip chart recorder. Through the use of this device, it was possible to measure the growth rate of grains and plants to an accuracy of plus or minus 0.001 inches per hour.

In January of 1967, I conducted an experiment in which this highly precise method of measuring growth rate was used to measure the effect of thought upon remotely located plants. The experiment was unique in that it coupled a highly scientific and accurate measuring technique with the prayer stimuli generated by two of the world's most gifted healers, Olga and Ambrose Worrall.

Plant Selection

The selection of the proper plant for use in the experiment turned out to be more of a problem than

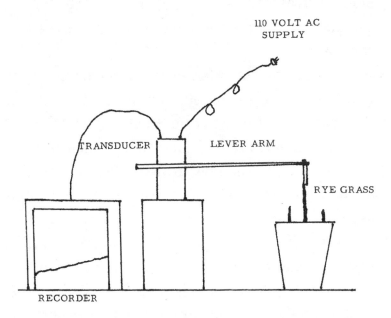

Figure 1 — Apparatus for measuring plant growth rate.

was anticipated. Initial experiments were performed on bean plants because they are sturdy and grow rapidly. As shown in Figure 1, the tip of the plant was attached to a counterbalanced lever arm, which, in turn, was connected to a Model 33-03 Brush Metripak Angular Position Transducer. The slightest motion of the lever arm is converted to an electrical signal which causes a deflection of the pen on a strip chart recorder. A wide range of accuracy could be achieved by adjusting the amplification of the recorder and the chart speed.

A plant growing at a constant rate generates a sloping straight line on the chart with the slope of the line directly proportional to the growth rate of the plant.

Initial experiments were conducted with bean plants. When these plants were properly watered, they had a rapid growth rate. However, it was found that the strip chart recorder did not measure the growth because the new growth always occurred at the tip of the plant above the point where the lever arm was attached.

After experimenting with a number of other plants, it was found that ordinary rye grass had all the necessary characteristics. It is sturdy and grows rapidly. In addition, it has the property of growing at the portion of the grass blade which is adjacent to the soil. Consequently, a lever arm attached to the tip of a blade of rye grass will measure total increase in length.

Experimental Procedure

In starting each test, rye grass seeds were placed in a 25-milliliter plastic beaker filled with a fertile soil. The seeds were planted 1/4 inch below the surface of the soil and were watered every morning with five milliliters of water. They began to sprout after two days and, after four days, the blades of grass were long enough to permit attachment of the lever arm to one of the sprouts. A small piece of Scotch tape provided the connecting link.

A number of preliminary experiments were performed on the effects of light on plant growth. The grass did not grow as rapidly in the dark as it did when exposed to fluorescent lighting. The growth rate trace was so sensitive that an irregularity was produced by merely turning the light switch on and off.

Ambrose and Olga Worrall visited Atlanta in the spring of 1967 to give a talk on their healing experiences to a local church group. I invited them to tour the research facility where I was employed and, while they were there, showed them the sensitive and accurate mechanism for measuring the

growth rate of plants. I asked if they would cooperate in a distant prayer experiment when they returned to their home in Baltimore, Maryland, some
600 miles away. They agreed to do so.

A few weeks later, my device was working perfectly and showed that the growth rate of a new
blade of rye grass had stabililzed at 6.25 mils per
hour (0.00625 inches/hr). During the night of February 3, the trace on the strip chart recorder was a
straight line with a constant slope. The straight
line continued with little or no deviation during the
day of February 4.

At 8:00 p.m. on the evening of February 4, I
called the Worralls and asked them to hold the plant
in their thoughts at their usual 9:00 p.m. prayer
time. They said they would do so. Their method of
praying for the sick was to visualize the subject as
being filled with light and energy, and being in a
state of perfect health.

Test Results

The next morning the trace on the strip chart
recorder, illustrated in Figure 2, was carefully examined. All through the evening until 9:00 p.m.,
the trace was a straight line with a slope which rep-
resented 6.25 mils per hour. At exactly 9:00 p.m. the
trace began to deviate upward and by 8:00 a.m. the

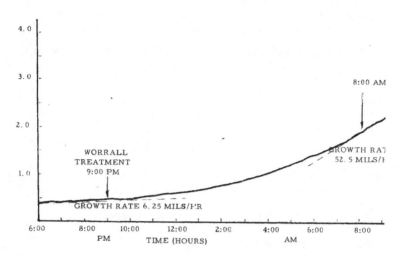

Figure 2—Effect of prayer on growth of rye grass

next morning showed that the rye grass blade was growing at a rate of 52.5 mils per hour, an increase of 840 percent! The experiment was continued for another forty-eight hours. During that time the growth rate decreased but never did get back to its original rate.

Discussion and Conclusions

The results of this experiment on the effect of thought on plants is highly significant. Similar tests with humans are usually inconclusive because of the number of variables involved. The thoughts and receptivity of the patient, the subject's environment, the temperature, and even the lighting conditions can influence the outcome of a test.

By selecting a plant as our biological system, we eliminated the effect of the test subject's thought process. The constant growth rate of the plant before the test indicates that steady state conditions were achieved.

During the experiment the door of the laboratory which housed the plant and the apparatus had been locked, the temperature was constant at 70-72 degrees F, the fluorescent lights were on continuously, and there was no known variable which could have caused such a dramatic increase in the growth rate of the rye grass. The evidence indicates that Ambrose and Olga Worrall, from a distance of 600 miles, produced an eight-fold increase in the growth rate of the rye grass.

In our contacts and discussions with the Worralls, we learned something about the mechanism of effective prayer. Olga told us she never permitted anyone to pray for her because, if it were not done properly, the prayer might worsen the condition being prayed for. She said that prayers should never recite or concentrate on the ailment or problem but should always describe or visualize the desired condition of perfect health.

Olga and Ambrose were in the habit of praying at 9:00 p.m. every evening for all the patients who had written or telephoned for help. They told

Genevieve Miller with Ambrose and Olga Worrall in front of laboratory where the rye grass experiment was conducted.

the patients to become perfectly quiet and relaxed at that time so they could receive the healing energies and thoughts that were being directed to them. Many healings resulted when this procedure was followed.

Even though Olga and Ambrose have now passed over, the tradition of a 9:00 p.m. healing is still being maintained by the healing team of the New Life Clinic.

8

Creative Turbulence

Olga Worrall visited Agnes Scott College in Atlanta, Georgia during January of 1974 to address students, faculty members, and visitors. One full day was devoted to tests designed to investigate Olga's unique abilities. The key experiment had the objective of determining whether or not some type of measurable energy is given off by a healer's hands. Dr. Philip Reinhart, who was head of the physics department at Agnes Scott College, participated in the tests.

Test Equipment

A cloud chamber, an apparatus originally developed by nuclear physicists for making visible the path of high energy nuclear particles, was used as the detector. The test device was an Atomic Laboratories Model 71850 laboratory cloud chamber. It consisted of a cylindrical glass chamber seven inches in diameter and five inches in height, which

51

has a sheet aluminum bottom and a viewing glass across the top. The unit is operated by covering the floor of the chamber with a 1/4-inch layer of alcohol and placing the chamber upon a flat block of dry ice.

When the surface of the alcohol is in contact with an enclosed volume of air, some of the alcohol molecules evaporate into the air to form a vapor. Equilibrium conditions are reached when the rate of evaporation from the surface of the liquid is just balanced by the rate of reentry of the alcohol molecules from the vapor into the liquid.

Chilling the bottom of the chamber by contact with dry ice creates a supersaturated zone in the chamber. When a charged nuclear particle, such as an alpha or beta ray, passes through the chamber, it ionizes molecules of air and produces a trail of positive and negative ions along its path. The alcohol vapor condenses on these nuclei and a visible trail, similar to the track of a high flying jet aircraft on a clear day, is created.

Tests at Agnes Scott College

During preliminary experiments, members of the investigating team placed their hands around the cloud chamber to see if they could influence the vapor zone. There was no discernable effect.

When Dr. Worrall performed the experiment, she placed her hands at the sides of the chamber without touching the glass, as illustrated in the photograph below. She then visualized energy flowing from her hands, much as she does when treating a patient. The observers saw a wave pattern develop in the supersaturated zone which, until she placed her hands in position, had been quite uniform in appearance. The waves were parallel to her hands and the direction of motion was perpendicular to the palms.

After several minutes, Dr. Worrall shifted her

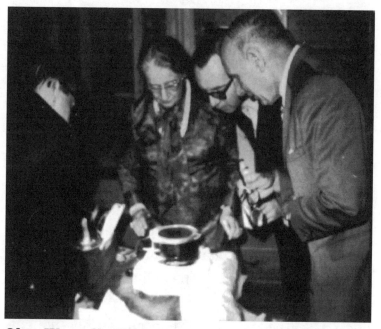

Olga Worrall stirring up waves in a cloud chamber. Dr. Miller is at the far right.

position ninety degreees to see if the pattern in the cloud chamber would be affected. The waves began to change direction and were soon moving perpendicularly to their original path.

Long Distance Test

On March 12, 1974, a follow-up experiment was conducted. A camera was mounted to enable photographs of the cloud chamber activity to be made. In addition, the experiment was designed to determine if Mrs. Worrall could affect the cloud chamber from a distance.

The cloud chamber was again in the physics laboratory at Agnes Scott College in Atlanta, Georgia, but Olga Worrall was in Baltimore, Maryland, some 600 miles away. The cloud chamber was prepared and the sensitivity was checked by inserting a radium 226 alpha source into the chamber and observing the condensed vapor trails generated by the alpha particles. Figure 3 is a photograph which was taken at that time. Except for the alpha tracks, only a fine mist, uniformly distributed, was visible.

After the cloud chamber had attained a steady state condition, a telephone call was made to Baltimore to let Olga know that all was in order and to ask her if, at 8:50 p.m., she would concentrate her thoughts and energies upon the cloud chamber. It was suggested that she mentally hold her hands at the sides of the chamber for several minutes and then change the orientation ninety degrees—as she did when she was actually present in the physics laboratory.

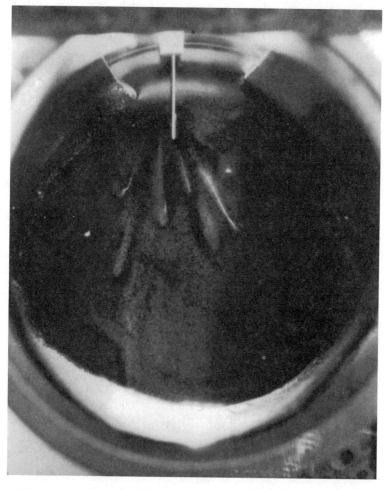

Figure 3—cloud chamber in stabilized condition. Streaks at top are from alpha particles emanating from radium test needle.

The members of the research team eagerly observed the cloud chamber as the critical time approached. At 8:53 p.m., a definite change occurred in the cloud chamber. The mist began to pulsate and dark waves were visible. The pattern

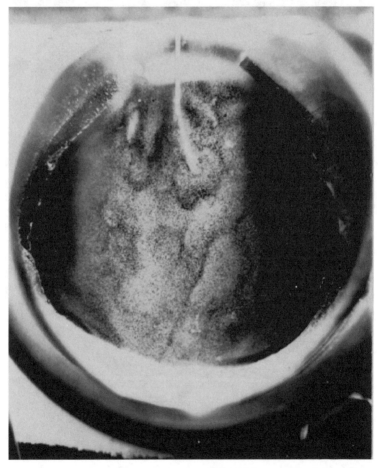

Figure 4—cloud chamber while Olga was focusing on it from 600 miles away. Note the turbulence in the heart of the mist.

was similar to that which might be seen in a pan of boiling gravy. Figure 4 is a photograph taken at the time. The pulsation continued for about seven minutes but never changed direction. Then the motion in the chamber gradually subsided.

A second telephone call was then made to Dr. Worrall to get a report of her mental impressions. She said she had been able to transfer her consciousness to the laboratory and had mentally placed her hands at the sides of the chamber, focusing her attention on producing motion in the chamber. She felt a cool sensation as if a cold breeze was flowing over her hands. She said that she did not shift the position of her hands during the experiment.

After the telephone conversation was concluded, Dr. Reinhart commented that it would be even more conclusive if the experiment could be repeated. Since the cloud chamber was already operating and stabilized, it was decided to call Mrs. Worrall and ask if she would again concentrate on the chamber. The experiment was repeated and the sensitive zone of the chamber again became turbulent as undulations, at a rate of about one per second, were perceived. A time interval of approximately eight minutes was required for the turbulence to subside after the second test.

Discussion and Conclusions

At the beginning of the first telephone conversation, Olga said, "You put the cloud chamber in a different room, didn't you? I had to look for it." She was correct—we did have the cloud chamber set up in a different room from where Olga had seen it when she was in Atlanta.

Olga also asked, "Who were the two ladies in the room? I had to screen out their thoughts before I could concentrate on the cloud chamber." This statement was also true; my wife Genevieve and a student assistant were observing the cloud chamber along with Dr. Reinhart and myself.

In a final telephone conversation with Dr. Worrall, we discussed the time interval required for the sensitive zone of the chamber to become quiescent after each experiment. Olga suggested that the cloud chamber had become charged with some type of energy, and a finite span of time was required for its dissipation. She also said that, in both local and distant healing, the energy acts on human beings much as it did in the cloud chamber—it churns up activity and stimulates cell repair and growth.

These experiments with the cloud chamber—a recognized and accepted research tool—have demonstrated scientifically that tangible energy does issue from the hands of healers and can stimulate targeted energy fields. The second experiment additionally proves that such healing energies can easily and instantly travel as much as 600 miles, or more, and still have an undiminished impact on the target.

These experiments also suggest that "thoughts are things"—and can have a remarkable impact on the phenomena of the physical world.

9

Measuring Healing Energies

The literature of scientific research contains references to an energy which cannot be detected by ordinary laboratory instruments. This energy, which is reported to emanate from the hands of certain individuals, accelerates the healing of wounds on mice[1], causes changes in enzyme systems[2] and increases the growth rate of plants and yeast cells[3]. There used to be doubt that such an energy existed because it would not register on thermometers, radiometers, thermocouples or other commonly used sensors.

One of the objectives of the research program sponsored by the Holmes Center for Research in Holistic Healing was to develop methods for detecting and measuring the energy which comes from the hands of individuals who, according to the literature, have healing abilities[4].

The principal test subject for the project was Dr. Olga Worrall.

Crystallization Effects

It was discovered that under controlled conditions, solutions of cupric chloride, a copper salt, are sensitive to the energies from a healer's hands. A small pool of cupric chloride solution (715 grams/liter) was pipetted onto each of two polyethylene discs. Dr. Worrall treated one specimen by holding her hands around it for three minutes. The second specimen served as a control.

After two days at room temperature (70-75 degrees F) and approximately 50 percent relative humidity, the specimen treated by Olga had crystallized in a coarse-grained, turquois-colored mono-

Figure 5—crystals formed from cupric chloride solutions. The crystal on the left was untreated; the one on the right changed in both color and texture after a three-minute treatment.

clinic structure. The untreated control specimen was also monoclinic but was fine-grained and was jade green in color. Figure 5 illustrates the difference in structure and color between the treated and control specimens.

Surface Tension of Water

It was suspected that the variation in the structure and color of the crystallized copper salt was caused by a difference in the properties of the water. Samples of distilled water which had been treated by a healer and untreated water were tested for viscosity, electrical conductivity, capacitance, re-

Fisher Model 20 Du Nuoy Tensiometer.

fractive index, infrared absorption, and surface tension. There were little or no differences in viscosity and refractive index. There were differences in electrical conductivity and capacitance but no consistent pattern could be established. The most significant differences were in the surface tension and infrared absorption.

The Du Nuoy type Tensiometer illustrated here was used to make the surface tension measurements. This instrument has a platinum-iridium ring suspended from a counter-balanced lever arm. The ring is immersed in the liquid being studied. The force necessary to separate the ring from the liquid is measured and read directly in dynes/cm.

Measuring the Energy from a Healer's Hands

The following procedure was developed to enable the test subject to transfer energy to water without direct contact.

The individual being tested holds the ends of two stainless steel rods 1/16 inch in diameter and seven inches long, one in each hand, and immerses the other ends of the rods in a beaker containing 100 milliliters of distilled water for exactly three minutes. Dr. Olga Worrall was tested while energizing a sample of distilled water. The surface tension of the water is measured before and after the treatment.

Olga Worrall energizing a sample of distilled water by visualizing healing energy flowing down the two stainless steel rods being held in her hands.

As energy is absorbed by the water, the attraction between adjacent molecules decreases and less force is required to withdraw the platinum-iridium tensiometer ring from the water. The difference between the before and after surface tension readings is a measure of the energy transferred from the test subject to the water.

The most significant feature of this procedure is that, for the first time, a method exists for quantitatively measuring the energy from a healer's hands.

Ambrose Worrall called the energy "paraelectricity," because it acts like electricity in flowing from a person with a high potential or energy level to a person or object at lower potential.

It is therefore recommended that the unit of quantity for healing energy be named a Worrall and that it be defined as the energy required to reduce the surface tension of 100 milliliters of distilled water from its normal value (72.4 dynes/cm at 68 degrees F) by 10 dynes/cm.

Table I summarizes the results of tests in which samples of water were energized and compared with control samples. The test subjects were Dr. Olga Worrall, Kathryn Hill, an Atlanta healer, and the author.

Table One
EFFECT OF PARAELECTRICITY
ON SURFACE TENSION OF WATER

TEST SUBJECT	SURFACE TENSION (DYNES/CM)	
	Before Treatment	After Treatment
Dr. Olga Worrall	70.1	62.97
Kathryn Hill	68.3	60.77
Dr. Robert Miller	74.6	71.17

Dr. Worrall and Kathryn Hill, recognized healers, reduced the surface tension of 100 milliliters of distilled water 7.2 and 7.6 dynes/cm. respectively. I produced a much smaller effect. These results, and the results of scores of additional tests with thirty or more individuals, indicate that quantitative data on the energy transferred from individuals to water may be obtained by measuring the changes in the surface tension.

Another significant conclusion that can be drawn from the results of these tests is that all humans have some paraelectricity or biomagnetic energy but those who have healing abilities are above average in their ability to lower the surface tension of water.

Properties of Water Treated with Magnets

In the middle 1800's in France, Henry Mesmer[5]

cured people with a variety of ailments by pointing magnets at the affected areas of the body. Reichenbach[6] also reported that magnets, as well as humans, give off some type of energy. He stated that, in a perfectly dark room, the sensitives he worked with could see light emanating from the poles of magnets.

Inasmuch as qualified healers such as Olga Worrall were not always available for testing, it was decided to investigate the effect of magnetic energy upon water and upon solutions of copper salts. In addition, magnetically energized water was tested for its effect upon the growth rate of plants.

The experiments which were conducted revealed that energy from a magnet will decrease the surface tension of water. A doughnut-shaped ferrite magnet three inches in diameter and one-half inch thick was immersed in 400 milliliters of water for sixteen hours. During that time the surface tension of the water decreased 12.2 dynes/cm.—from 72.6 dynes/cm. to 60.4 dynes/cm. The surface tension of water in a control beaker, which had no contact with a magnet, was unchanged.

A cupric chloride solution was exposed to a magnetic field of 4500 gauss for fifteen minutes. After two days at room temperature the crystals from the solution which had been exposed to the magnet were turquois blue, while the crystals from the control solution, which had not been exposed, were jade green. This same color pattern was obtained in the crystallization tests with healer-treated water.

Additional tests were conducted to determine the effect of water treated by a magnet and water treated by a healer upon the growth of rye grass. Exactly 25 rye grass seeds were placed in each of six plastic cups filled with potting soil. Holes were punched in the bottoms and each cup was placed on a saucer. Water was placed in the saucers so the seeds obtained their water at a uniform rate by capillary action. Two of the cups were watered every day with Atlanta tap water, two with tap water which had been treated by Dr. Worrall thirty days before, and two with tap water which had been exposed to a magnetic field of 4500 gauss for sixteen hours.

At the end of four days 8 percent of the seeds in the control cup had sprouted, 36 percent of the seeds in the cup with the healer-treated water had sprouted, and 68 percent sprouting occurred in the cup with the magnetically energized water.

After eight days the length of each blade of grass was carefully measured. The average height of the control blades was 2.6 inches, the blades that grew in the healer-treated water averaged 2.9 inches, and the grass blades that grew in the magnetically-energized water had an average length of 3.6 inches, 28.6 percent more than the control. If growth rate can be equated to healing, the results indicate that healing energies emanate from magnets. Indeed, this was one of the claims made by Mesmer in the middle 1800's.

It was anticipated that the healer-treated water and the magnetically-treated water would increase the growth rate of the rye grass by approximately the same amount. The test results indicate that the water treated by Dr. Olga Worrall was not as effective as the water treated with a magnet. However, Dr. Worrall had energized the water used in the experiment some 30 days before the test was made. This raised the question as to whether the water had lost energy prior to its being used in the experiment. The following test on the stability of energized water demonstrated that the water gradually gives up its energy to the surrounding environment.

Two hundred and fifty milliliters of distilled water were energized by immersing two ceramic magnets, 3/4 of an inch in diameter and 1/8 of an inch thick, in the water and stirring the water for fifteen minutes. This resulted in a lowering of the

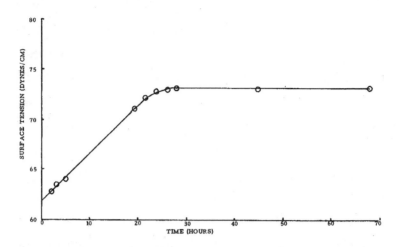

Figure 6 — Energy dissipation rate of water that has been treated magnetically.

surface tension from 72.4 to 62.2 dynes/cm. The open glass beaker was then exposed to a normal room environment (70-75 degrees F) for seventy hours while surface tension of the water was measured at periodic intervals. Figure 6 is a plot of the change in surface tension during that time period. The surface tension of the water gradually increased and, by the end of twenty-four hours, was back to its normal range of 72-73 dynes/cm.

This result was not surprising when we consider the fact that healer-energized or magnetically-energized water accelerates the growth rate of plants. This happens because energy from the water is absorbed by the plant. The knowledge that energized water loses its energy with time also explains why the water which had been energized by Olga Worrall thirty days before it was tested on a plant was not as effective as fresh magnetically energized water.

Russian scientists[7] report that strong magnetic fields affect the hydrogen bonding of water. Experiments conducted on this program and also by other investigators[8] demonstrated that the energy from a healer's hands also changes the hydrogen bonding of water. Each molecule of water has two atoms of hydrogen and one of oxygen. Hydrogen bonding occurs when an atom of hydrogen is attracted by rather strong forces to two oxygen atoms instead of only one. Since the hydrogen atom has only one stable orbital electron and can form only one covalent bond, the hydrogen bond is largely ionic in character with the hydrogen atom oscillating between the two oxygen atoms involved in the bonding[9].

Specimens of distilled water and distilled water which had been energized by Dr. Olga Worrall were analyzed by infrared absorption using an infrared spectrophotometer equipped with an internal reflectance cell. The infrared light beam passes through a crystal which is immersed in the water and is reflected from the surface of the water many times, giving a much higher degree of accuracy

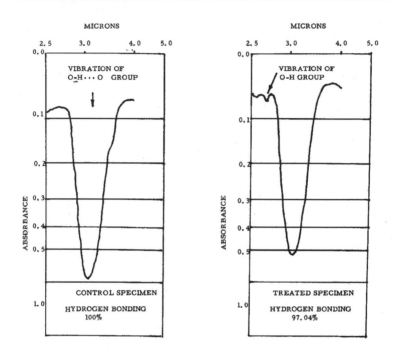

Figure 7—Infrared absorption spectra of distilled water (left) and water energized by Dr. Olga Worrall (right).

than is obtainable by simple absorption techniques. The infrared analyses were performed by Dr. Edward Brame of Wilmington, Delaware.

Figure 7 shows the infrared absorption traces for the control and the energized water specimens. The hydrogen bonding peak occurs in the 2.8-3.2 micron wave length band. The left hand control trace has a single peak in the hydrogen bonded wave length. This indicates that all the molecules of water are hydrogen-bonded to adjacent molecules.

The trace for the energized specimen has a large peak in the 2.8-3.2 hydrogen bonding range but has a second small peak in the 2.6-2.7 micron range. The ratio of the height of the hydrogen bonding peak to the sum of the heights of both peaks, expressed as percent, shows that only 97.04 percent of the hydrogen in the treated water is hydrogen bonded. The results of these infrared absorption tests, conducted on a standard laboratory instrument, demonstrate that energy from a healer's hands produces changes in the bonding and the molecular structure of water.

Experiment at Lourdes

There is an interesting sequel to this research project. Dr. Worrall and I were invited to present the results of our experiments at a conference on healing at King's College at the University of London in England. This gave us an opportunity to test a theory I had evolved—that the healings which were reported to occur at healing shrines like Lourdes were due to energy in the spring waters at the shrines.

I took my tensiometer to Europe with me and, after the London conference, Olga, Genevieve, and I traveled to Lourdes in southern France. There we were able to get a sample of water directly from the spring at the spot where Bernadette first saw her vision of Mary. The basilica at Lourdes rises over a beautiful setting located at the base of the Pyrennes mountains, almost on the border between France and Spain.

Every night the thousands of pilgrims who come to Lourdes for healing and inspiration parade through the streets with torches singing *Ave Maria*. The whole town is charged with energy. One evening Genevieve and I marched with the pilgrims and, as we joined in the singing, I could feel the hair rise on the back of my neck.

One of the healing ceremonies involves immersion of the patient in a huge stone tub filled with water from the spring. The patient strips to the waist and, clad only in shorts, is pulled backward and immersed in the cold water by two attendants. At the same time a prayer for healing, in the native language of the patient, is recited. Although I did not have an ailment that needed curing, I participated in the ceremony and can testify to the fact that it was a peak experience.

Dr. Theodore Mangiapan, the medical director at Lourdes, unlocked the glass panel which protects the outlet of the spring and permitted me to fill a flask with water directly from the spring. Within two hours after obtaining the sample, I checked the

The basilica at Lourdes.

Dr. Mangiapan, the Lourdes medical director, between Dr. Olga Worrall and Dr. Robert N. Miller.

The grotto where Bernadette saw her vision.

The source of healing water at Lourdes.

surface tension of the water with the tensiometer. Much to my surprise, the surface tension was 72 dynes/cm, the same as water from taps in the hotel. Dr. Mangiapan had told me that other scientists had also checked the Lourdes water and could find no special properties.

Although the results seem to be negative, they are actually highly significant. They indicate that the healings which occur at Lourdes are probably due to three factors: 1) the accumulation of psychic energy from the millions of devoted pilgrims who have visited the shrine through the years, 2) there may be healing energies (angelic or divine) that do not affect the physical properties of water, and 3) expectations in the subconscious minds of the ailing supplicants who are brought to Lourdes. If a patient firmly believed he would be healed as the result of being immersed in the sacred waters, the heightened energy field which one can physically sense, plus the shock of the immersion in the icy cold bath, could cause the miracle to occur.

Implications

The decrease in the hydrogen bonding in water treated by a healer indicates that the energy level of the water has increased. When we recall that 65 to 70 percent of the human body is water, we can see why a laying-on-of-hands treatment by a healer like Olga Worrall could energize a sick person and accelerate the healing of physical ailments.

Reproducible results from experiments with the energy from a healer's hands or from magnets require strict control of all of the variables involved. The energy is absorbed and conducted by various materials in unpredictable ways. The introduction of metal stirring rods or plastic beakers into the experiment causes a variation in the results obtained. The use of glass containers and stirring rods is mandatory.

The results of the experiments described in this chapter indicate that a primary energy, different from the energies recognized by modern science, is emitted from the hands of healers and by magnets. The energies from both sources cause decreases in the surface tension of water, change the structure and color of crystals from cupric chloride solutions, change the hydrogen bonding of water, and accelerate the growth rate of rye grass.

It is hoped that the procedures and techniques which were developed in this project will be used to further study the nature of the healing energy and to determine how it may be generated, stored, transferred and used with maximum efficiency.

Conclusions

Until now, science and religion have been in opposite camps about prayer and healing. Science has believed that divine intercession defies physical laws; religion has labeled them "miracles" and insisted that they be accepted on faith.

The experiments reported in this chapter give us a basis for closing the gap. Scientific methods and measurements have now been used to understand what is actually happening in the miracles we call prayer and healing. This should not be seen as a substitute for faith, but rather as a revelation that enhances and strengthens our faith.

Properly pursued, these experiments—and others like them—let us analyze, step by step, these tremendous and remarkable "miracles in the making."

10

The Role of the Mind in Healing

Sick persons who are the recipients of prayer treatments frequently show dramatic improvement. Whether this is coincidental or the direct result of the treatments has not been conclusively established.

In 1883, for example, Francis Galton compared the life expectancies of prayerful people, such as priests and nuns, and secular people, such as doctors and lawyers.[13] He concluded that persons who pray or are prayed for do not have a longer life span than others. In 1934, however, Dr. Alexis Carrel[14], after studying spontaneous healings of many diseases throughout his professional life, reported that a state of prayer is indispensable to the occurrence of the phenomena. Finally, a study on the efficacy of prayer, conducted by Joyce and Weldon[15] in 1964, showed a slight statistical advantage in favor of the prayed-for group.

The acceptance by the medical community of

the benefits of prayers for the sick is illustrated by the fact that Harvard Medical School recently sponsored a symposium on spiritual healing. Dr. Howard Benson of Harvard Medical School stated that, "When patients pray, beneficial physiological changes occur. Prayer procedures should be modified according to the patient's religious beliefs."

At the conference, a Dr. Bird reported on the results of a study with 393 coronary care patients. They were divided into two groups. One group was prayed for while the other group was not. A double blind procedure was used—patients did not know which group they were in.

A statistical analysis of results showed the prayed-for group to be healthier than the control group at the conclusion of the test period. The most significant result was that twelve patients in the not-prayed-for group had to have surgery, oxygen or mechanical assistance to stay alive. No special help was required for any patient in the prayed-for group.

The objectives of the 1976 research program sponsored by the Holmes Center for Research in Holistic Healing included (a) clarifying the mental and physical processes involved in remote mental healing and (b) measuring the effectiveness of Science of Mind practitioners and other mental healers.

Test Procedure

The following test was used to determine, on a statistical basis, whether or not spiritual mind treatments and other forms of mental healing have a significant effect upon the recovery of patients. The experiment, designed with the aid of two medical doctors and a medical statistician, involved ninety-six hypertension patients and eight healers. Half of the patients were used as controls, and each patient in the other half was assigned to one of eight healers.

The healers were selected on the basis of their reputation for being successful in their healing treatments. Four were Science of Mind practitioners, one was a Presbyterian minister, one a Church of Christ minister, one the director of the Seventh Sense Institute, and the eighth was Olga Worrall.

The study was conducted by a double blind procedure designed so that neither the patients nor the physician knew which patients received the remote mental healing treatments until the experiment was completed. Improvement in the condition of the patients was judged on the basis of physiological parameters which give a numerical readout, i.e., diastolic blood pressure, systolic blood pressure, heart beat rate and weight.

Normal medical treatment was continued in all cases.

After the conclusion of the treatment period, the pre- and post-treatment data for the patients was analyzed by a medical statistician using an "analysis of variance" computer program.[16]

Treatment Methods

Each healer who participated in the program was asked to make a tape which described in detail his or her exact thoughts and feelings while they were administering their healing treatments. The following descriptions of healing procedures were summarized from the tapes.

Dr. Olga Worrall

"In requests for absent healing, a patient either writes me or phones me and asks for help. If the request comes to me by mail, then I hold the letter in my hand and psychometrize the letter, which means I try to find out just what is the real cause of the problem and the location (on the body) of the problem. I then read the letter and, when I have finished reading, I mentally project the healing energy toward this point. As far as I'm concerned, the energy has intelligence. However, I do direct it to the part of the person that is not functioning properly, and I visualize the energy stimulating the body and bringing it back on course so once again the pattern of perfection can manifest. If the problem is a tumor, I visualize the tumor dissolving and being carried away by the body, and if there is a mental disorder I visualize the peace of God coming into that soul's being."

Dr. Vetura Papke
Science of Mind Practitioner

"Dr. Ernest Holmes gave to us five steps of treatment. The first is a recognition of God. The second step is a unification with God and the third, realization—realizing the truth concerning the so-called problem. The fourth step is thanksgiving and the fifth, release—letting it go.

"I have found that since I have used these five steps, many of my treatments or prayers have been answered. I believe that we are surrounded with and are immersed in a mind, an intelligence—an intelligence that responds to us according to our acceptance of it."

The following spiritual mind treatment by Dr. Papke applies the above principles:

"We now join together in consciousness knowing that God is all the beauty of the universe, all of the love, the harmony, the peace, the wholeness—

all of the life essence in all things. Since I am created in the image and after the likeness of God, therefore I have within me all His potential.

"In the realization of this, I speak my word for W. M. (name of patient), and in speaking my word I set the law of mind in motion for him to bring into his experience his good, to know his mind is open, receptive only to infinite intelligence and nothing else. He literally lets the mind of God flow through his mind. His body is the temple of the living spirit, of Almighty God, and the activating power of God moving in and through him, in every atom, every cell, every organ of his body reveals this truth, the perfection of God, that is there.

"I declare there is no suggestion, no belief in this disease which seems to operate through him. This is an illusion. The only power given to it is his acceptance. As this law is set in motion it neutralizes all negation. What needs to be healed is healed. What needs to be changed is changed regardless of appearances and anyone's opinion, including his own. Since his spiritual self is perfect, created in the image and after the likeness of God, every evidence to the contrary is completely erased and dissolved.

"As the physical self must reflect that which is within and manifest perfection, therefore, the truth is, he is whole, perfect, and complete, for with God all things are possible.

"Therefore, as this great law of mind is set in motion, I now give thanks, grateful thanks, that this word has set a new cause in motion, that there is not only a power but a loving presence that does respond, that loves and cares for him and for each one. In this assurance I release this prayer into the law, knowing it is done now, right now, and so it is. Amen."

The procedures used by the three other Science of Mind practitioners who participated in this program were similar to this one used by Dr. Papke.

Reverend Alex Holmes
Presbyterian minister

The Reverend Alex Holmes visualizes his patient as being in a state of perfect health, while he verbally affirms that the healing is taking place.

Reverend Richard Batzler
United Church of Christ minister

The Reverend Richard Batzler uses the following procedure in his healing treatments:

1. Relaxation.
2. Deep breathing.
3. Centering consciousness on God, by silently

saying and hearing the word, "God, God, God."

4. The centering moves, in an ebb and flow rhythm, to a visualization of the patient, then back to God. This step in the process continues for five to ten minutes.

Benjamin Bibb

Seventh Sense Institute

Benjamin Bibb describes his procedure as "televisual healing," and communicates with the subconscious mind of the patient through visual symbols. He outlines his method as follows:

"Contact the inner mind of the subject and observe the true nature of the injury or malfunction.

"Use mental pictures to show the subject's inner mind how to correct the problem.

"Supply mental energy and instruct the subject's inner mind how to obtain the energy necessary for it to perform and sustain the healing.

"See the subject perfectly healed, then break contact gently and give no further thought at that time, although the treatment may be repeated later."

Assignment

The patients were assigned to the program at the rate of four per week. On a random basis, two of the patients were assigned to the control group and the other two were assigned to one of the eight healers for treatment within the next week. The healer was given the patient's initials, sex, age, general health problem, and location. Whenever possible, two male and two female patients were assigned to the program each week.

This procedure was followed until ninety-six patients were allocated to the program, and each healer had treated six people.

Statistical Results

The pre- and post-treatment data were taken from the medical records of the doctor who was treating the patient. The data were then analyzed using the "Analysis of Variance and Covariance Including Repeated Measures" methodology of the Health Sciences Computing Facility of the University of California. First, the pre- and post-treatment data for each parameter for the healer-tested group and for the control group were compared. Then the results of the four healers for whom the largest number of sets of post-treatment data were available were compared with the average of the control group. The final analysis was based on the number of patients who improved, instead of the numerical change for each parameter.

Table I summarizes the systolic blood pressure data for the patients treated by the four healers. The systolic pressure is the reading obtained when the heart is contracting and the blood is under maximum pressure. The average decrease in systolic blood pressure for the control group was 9.2 units. The average decrease for the patients treated by the four healers was 12.9 units. The statistical probability of error was 1 in 70.

Table One
COMPARISON OF AVERAGES OF PRE-AND POST-TREATMENT SYSTOLIC BLOOD PRESSURES

	C.G.	#1	#2	#3	#4
Pre-Treatment	138.3	137.5	160.5	147.0	137.5
Post-Treatment	130.1	123.0	149.0	134.8	124.3
Change	-9.2	-14.5	-11.5	-12.5	-13.2
	(p=.014)				

Table II compares the pre- and post-treatment data for the diastolic (lowest) blood pressures for the control and the treated groups. The average drop for the control group was 5.5 units; for the healer-treated group, it was 5.75 units.

Table Two
COMPARISON OF AVERAGES OF PRE-AND POST-TREATMENT DIASTOLIC BLOOD PRESSURES

	C.G.	#1	#2	#3	#4
Pre-Treatment	92.6	96.5	87.5	93.5	95.5
Post-Treatment	87.1	87.5	83.5	88.5	87.5
Change	-5.5	-9.0	-4.0	-5.0	-5.0

(p=.087)

Tables III and IV compare the changes in weight and pulse rates of the patients. The results were mixed and not statistically significant.

Table III indicates a uniform weight loss in the patients treated by the healers, with the exception of

Table Three
COMPARISON OF PRE-AND POST-TREATMENT WEIGHTS (in pounds)

	C.G.	#1	#2	#3	#4
Pre-Treatment	187.3	180.0	267.3	174.0	175.0
Post-Treatment	188.7	179.0	282.0	172.8	172.8
Change	+1.4	-1.0	+14.7	-1.2	-2.2

(p=.0138)

healer #2. One of this healer's patients gained a considerable amount of weight, which skewed the results dramatically.

Table IV compares pulse rates for the control and the healer-treated groups. The average change for the control group was a decrease of 5.0 beats per minute; the pulse rate in the healer-treated patients dropped an average of 2.5 beats per minute.

Table Four
COMPARISON OF PRE-AND POST-TREATMENT PULSE RATES

	C.G.	#1	#2	#3	#4
Pre-Treatment	83.5	86.0	73.5	75.5	88.0
Post-Treatment	78.5	79.0	80.5	75.5	78.0
Change	-5.0	-7.0	+7.0	0.0	-10.0

The biggest difference between the control group and the treated patients occurred when we compared the number of patients in each category that showed improvement. According to this index, a patient was considered improved if two or more measurements in the parameter group improved by the end of the treatment period. These results are summarized in Table V. The statistical analysis for this table was made using Fisher's Exact Test Method[16].

Table Five
HEALTH STATUS

	Better	Worse	% Better
Control Group	14	5	73.7
Treated Group	11	1	92.3
	(p=.013)		

Discussion

An analysis of the treatment procedures used by the eight healers who participated in this study reveals that the four Science of Mind practitioners used the same general method. This process involved four steps:

1. Relaxation.

2. Attunement to a higher power.

3. A visualization and/or affirmation of the patient being in a state of perfect health.

4. An expression of thanks.

While some of the healers concluded their treatment in just a few minutes, one spent approximately ten minutes affirming the perfect health of each patient. Three of the healers stressed the visualization step, and two seemed to make mental contact with the patient and received impressions as to the nature of his or her health problem.

Not all of the healers who used the Science of Mind procedure outlined above achieved the same degree of success. This suggests that the effectiveness of a healing treatment depends upon factors such as the personal and physiological characteristics of the healers—and the characteristics of the patients—as well as upon the use of an effective procedure.

The results of this study indicate that four of the eight healers who participated in it clearly were effective in causing improvements in the health of their patients over and above that which could be expected on the basis of normal medical treatment. Three of the four were Science of Mind practitioners. The fourth was Olga Worrall, whose method of healing from a distance is similar to the Science of Mind procedure.

Discussions with the healers participating in this program revealed that few of their patients register instantaneous healings—as the result of a single treatment. For difficult cases, most healers continue their treatments over a period of time. This tends to suggest that each treatment produces a beneficial effect in the patient but, for best results, should be repeated. Ideally, post-treatment data should be obtained within a few days after each treatment.

It is interesting to note that three of the healers had a perfect score in terms of patient improvement, with 100 percent of their patients showing improvement, as compared with 73.7 percent of the patients in the control group. Olga Worrall was one of the three registering a perfect score.

An Hypothesis

How is it possible for the concentrated thoughts of a healer to produce results of improved health in another person many miles away? The underlying philosophy of mental healing procedures suggests the following hypothesis:

God, or the Creator, may be defined as the sum of the universe and its associated energies. Being a part of this total, every individual is a part of God and has creative powers. The universe is made up of energy in various states of condensation. This energy, especially in its finer states, responds to thought. As a result, if a healer or prayer group visualizes a sick person in a state of perfect health, this image tends to manifest in the body of the patient.

Conclusions

Two of the parameters tested in this experiment—the decrease in systolic blood pressure and the overall improvement of patients—demonstrate beyond any statistical doubt that healing prayers do work. These results also prove that a) a healing prayer can be transmitted to the patient from a far distance, and b) that it is not necessary for the healer to know the patient—or even his or her name.

The fact that eight healers and ninety-six patients were used in this experiment also indicates that the potential for such healing is far more widespread than we realize. Almost all of the patients who were treated by healers demonstrably improved, as opposed to less than three-fourths of the patients in the control group.

11

What the Experts Say

In the spring of 1975, the Church of Religious Science in Los Angeles sponsored a symposium on healing that drew together some remarkable people—and their insights.

Famed actor Robert Young—everybody's favorite parent on *Father Knows Best*—served as moderator and master of ceremonies. At that time, he was playing the role of Marcus Welby, M.D. on the popular television show of the same name. The speakers were Dr. Carl Simonton, Dr. Marcel Vogel, Gloria Swanson, Cleve Baxter, and myself.

Robert Young, with his humor and charm, had the capacity crowd of more than 500 in a good natured and anticipatory mood when he began to introduce the speakers.

Dr. Carl Simonton
An oncologist and radiation treatment specialist, Dr. Carl Simonton told of his experience with

cancer patients. He noted that a certain percentage of them improved and recovered although their symptoms seemed to be similar to those of patients who did not improve. This puzzled him, so he began to make an intensive study of the improving patients, to see if he could find a common denominator. In talking with the patients and reviewing their medical history, he discovered that their mental attitude seemed to be a significant factor. Most of those who expected to get better did improve.

Over a period of many months, Dr. Simonton developed a meditation and visualization procedure which not only enabled patients to become optimistic but which also greatly accelerated the healing process.

He told his patients to go to a quiet, peaceful spot three times a day and imagine themselves to be in a forest, or by the side of a lake under idyllic conditions. They were then to visualize the white cells of the blood destroying and absorbing the tumor cells. They were to continue this for a minimum time period of ten minutes. The recommended times for carrying out this procedure were immediately after awakening in the morning, once around noon, and the last thing at night before going to sleep. After each session, they were to release the problem completely and not think about it until the next meditation period. In all cases the usual treatment of radiation and chemotherapy was continued.

Dr. Simonton kept a careful record of those patients who followed these instructions. He discovered that tumors began to shrink and disappear at an accelerated rate. He showed the audience at the symposium color slides of massive tumors on patients shrinking month by month. After seeing slides for three or four patients the audience was awed by the significance of what they had just seen and heard. Here was a non-surgical method for controlling and, in some cases, curing cancer!

What Dr. Simonton had actually developed was a very effective prayer procedure. It is similar to the procedures used by both Olga Worrall and the Science of Mind practitioners who participated in the mental healing experiment described in chapter 10.

Cleve Baxter

The next speaker was Cleve Baxter, director of the Baxter School for Lie Detection in Manhattan and a former interrogation specialist with the Central Intelligence Agency. He told about his research with plants.

Baxter said it all started when his secretary

bought two plants because she thought something green was needed in the office. On February 2, 1966, Cleve was watering the plants and became curious as to how long it would take the water to get from the roots into the leaves. Since a lie detector measures electrical resistance, he attached the electrodes of a lie detector unit to a leaf. He figured that when the water got to the leaf its electrical resistance would decrease and the tracing on the graph paper would rise. But it didn't happen that way at all. Instead of going up, the pen tracing went down. Cleve was startled as he watched the pen make a trace which was typical of a human reaction.

"I wasn't about to be outdone by a plant," Cleve told us. "I thought if this plant wants to show me a people-like recording, I'll use people rules on it. In conventional lie detector work the best reactions are noted when the subject feels a threat to his well being.

Cleve figured that putting a leaf of the plant in a cup of hot coffee ought to be a pretty good threat. So he tried it. But the tracing drifted downward which, Cleve said, with a person would indicate complete boredom—as if to say, "If that's the best you can do, Buddy, forget about it." He then wiggled the wires and did everything he could to explain the graphical pattern. Finally, he became exasperated and decided to burn the leaf.

The dramatic moment is best expressed in Cleve's words. "I wasn't touching the plant or desk in any way. I was about ten feet from it. At the very moment I *thought* about burning the plant, the pen jumped right off the graph. The timing was so precise it seemed that the plant had read my mind."

Cleve knew better than to run out on Times Square yelling, "A plant has read my mind." He didn't want to be scooped up with a net by the men in white; he had his scientific reputation to protect. So, for the next three years he made repeated tests under rigorous scientific conditions. Only after he got reproducible results with different plants and with different observers conducting machine-run experiments did he write up a scientific paper.

Cleve found that plants react most violently to the termination of life, so he devised an experiment where batches of live brine shrimp were dropped into boiling water by a machine in a random, unpredictable manner. He put the machine into operation and, in an adjacent room, connected a lie detector to a plant. Then he started the strip chart recorders on the polygraph and on the shrimp dumping mechanism and left the area. Afterward, when he compared the traces from the machine and from the plant he found that, in every case, the plants had reacted violently at the precise instant the batches of brine shrimp were dropped into the boiling water. The experiment completely eliminated the human element and demonstrated that there is a connecting link between living matter.

Cleve conducted hundreds of experiments with many types of plants. His data indicate that they react to their environments and to their owners. Apparently plants can read minds, can remember, and can establish emotional relationships with people.

In one amazing experiment, six men entered a room in which there were two philodendron plants. One of the men tore one of the plants from its pot and stamped on it. Later, Baxter attached a polygraph to the remaining plant and the six men were brought back into the room, one at a time. When the "killer" entered the room the philodendron plant identified him with a violent and dramatic reaction.

Cleve tried to block the communication signals by shielding his plants with a Faraday screen. This is a metal shell which intercepts all types of electromagnetic radiation. He also tried lead-lined containers. Still, the communication signals reached the plants. The results of Cleve Baxter's work indicated that this ability to respond to human emotions is a primary perception which all plants exhibit.

All of Cleve Baxter's work is fascinating but the most significant indication of his results is that a life signal, or a communication link, may connect all of creation. Cleve is of the opinion that, in all probability, this perception is common to everything alive in the world.

Dr. Marcel Vogel

An IBM scientist, Dr. Marcel Vogel had been observing the formation of crystals from molten salts and from saturated solutions under a microscope and discovered that he could influence the pattern of the precipitated crystals by his thoughts. He showed color photographs of some of his results; the most astounding one was a clearly delineated cross which resulted from his concentrating on a mental image of a cross while the crystalization was occurring.

Gloria Swanson

The legendary actress called upon the members of the audience to pursue a "recollection of things spiritual" in their lives. She said that the one bright spot in the modern story of humanity is the growing enthusiasm of those who are seeking spiritual insights and truths. It is not just individuals who need healing, she declared, but the planet as a whole. This is something that cannot be done unless we call on the Creator to help us.

Dr. Olga Worrall

Olga Worrall, in her part of the program, held

Speakers at the symposium were Dr. Marcel Vogel, Gloria Swanson, Robert Young, and Olga Worrall; Dr. Carl Simonton, Cleve Baxter, Dr. Ballantine Henley, Dr. Robert N. Miller, and a church officer.

her listeners spellbound as she described some of her healing experiences.

"I was just a little girl when my parents discovered that I had this healing ability. I did it automatically; it was just part of me. We can liken this to a pianist—in the beginning the fingering is so important and then, without recognizing the fact, this type of exercise is no longer needed. The fingers know what they are to do. And so it is with one who is being used as a channel. I have a constant awareness of the presence of God—an inner knowing that the power is available. All I have to do is to plug into the source of supply.

"I remember as a child being asked to put my hands on someone who was sick. I would just naturally say, 'Please God, heal so and so—thank you, Jesus,' and that was the end of it. It just happened.

"To use an example, as a housewife I have a toaster. Unless I plug it into the source of supply, it won't work. The source of supply, or energy, is there—it's available at a moment's notice. The person has to do his proper part, which is plugging into the electrical connection. This is what healers do—they plug into the source of supply automatically.

"Sometimes I picture the condition desired, or I may say The Word, always with gratitude and thanksgiving for all good that is manifesting. As soon as I read a letter from a person who has a need, I immediately begin to send healing. If I get a call on the telephone, I immediately begin to send healing. I do not beseech or beg God; I know that only God knows that which is good for His creation. However, little ol' me must keep reminding myself of God's power. Too often in our agony we forget about God and His love for us. Prayers are reminders and should be indulged in.

"A healer must clear his or her mind of all anxiety, negative thoughts and concerns before he can become a clear carrier for this great power that flows from only one source, and that is God.

"I would like to share with you a few healings. After a lecture in Rochester, New York, a doctor approached me timidly and whispered in my ear that he had brought with him one of his patients, a young girl. He then told me that she had reacted violently to a new drug which caused her mouth to be covered with blisters and sores extending even into her stomach. There was nothing that he or his colleagues could prescribe that would counteract the medication.

"I placed my hands on the child's head for a few moments of prayer, thanking God for his healing power that was now manifesting in this child's body. The next morning the doctor phoned to tell me that, almost at once upon her return to the hospital, the child fell into a sound sleep. In the morning she awakened and was free of all blisters and sores—her mouth was healthy again. The doctor confessed to me that he felt that only God could have helped the child. Because of this experience, the doctor will be a great channel for God's healing energy. Incidentally, I gave him a lesson on how to think when praying.

"A woman who lives a good distance from Baltimore, at the suggestion of her surgeon, attended one of the healing services that I give at the Mt. Washington Methodist Church. He told her to come to me for spiritual comfort for she was about to face a serious operation for cancer of the back. As she was telling me her story I became aware of the healing energy in my hands, which became very hot. I immediately placed my hands on the area of her back which was diagnosed as being cancerous, visualizing this healing energy or 'paraelectricity' pouring into her body. I remained mentally quiet for a few minutes to let it settle. I perceived that something was taking place, and suggested that the woman have the doctor postpone the operaton for a month. The woman replied that, although she had felt my hands literally burning up her back, she could not interfere with the scheduled operation because seventeen doctors were involved. It was scheduled for the following Monday. I then informed her that the doctor would not find what he expected when he operated on her.

"Several months later the woman came to me to report that, two days after the operation, the doctor came into her room, brought up a chair to her bedside and asked her to tell him what I had to say when she had come to see me. She told him that I had told her that the operation should be postponed for a month and that healing was already taking place and that there was no need for an operation.

"The doctor then told the woman that he had witnessed his first miracle. He told her that when he operated he found that scar tissue was already forming, and that the cancer cells, when placed under the microscope, looked as though they had been burned up. The edges were curled up like cooked oysters. All he did was clean up that area. He told her that, indeed, within a month there would have been no need for an operation. Mother Nature would have removed the dead cells.

"Recently I received a call from a minister who had just been admitted to the hospital. The doctors diagnosed his problem as a kidney cyst and were planning to operate. He was asking for my healing prayers. As I prayed, I saw a perfect kidney. Then I thought, 'Why not include the other one as well, so I did.' I saw them free of all disease and mentally directed the energy to the kidneys. I advised the minister to insist on further tests before permitting the operation to be performed. This he did. Further X-rays and tests showed both kidneys to be healthy, the cause of the problem was gone, and there was no need for further doctoring. I did not touch the minister. I was not in his presence. This was done from a distance or, as we term it, by absent healing. In the laboratory we experimented with a cloud chamber and you know what happened there. Results were obtained both with touch and from 600 miles away.

"Recently, a husband called me on the telephone to tell me that his wife was expecting a baby and that the doctor thought a Cæsarean section would be necessary. I said to him, 'Well, I'll keep her in my prayers.' I snuck up on this one: I visualized a perfect passage for the baby. The next day the husband called to inform me that, as his wife was being wheeled into the operating room, she experienced a sharp pain and suddenly the baby came into the world. The father exclaimed, 'I almost delivered my baby daughter.' The baby is in perfect health, as is the mother. The doctors are baffled and one stated, 'Mother Nature pulled a fast one on us.' The doctor has a keen sense of humor. Mother Nature can indeed pull fast ones on us if we will cooperate with nature with our thoughts and our prayers.

"Several years ago, I met a woman at a meeting I hadn't seen for two years. I was so happy to see her that I put my hands around her and gave her a hug and a squeeze. After the meeting was over she confided in me that she had suffered for several years with pains in her neck and shoulders which her doctor was unable to help her with, other than with pain-killing medication. She said that when I placed my arm around her shoulders she felt terrific heat and an electric current seemed to go through her body. She went to her seat and within minutes realized that, for the first time in several years, she was free of all pain. Two years later, no discomfort had returned—she feels wonderful."

Olga Worrall summarized the results of the experiments I had conducted with her and with Ambrose by stating:

"The most important finding of our research to date is the confirmation that healing energies do exist, and can be controlled and directed through the proper application of scientific principles. Energies are transferred from the healer to the patient on both physical and nonphysical levels. Healing energies cause changes in the surface tension of water and the electrical characteristics of plants. The mental processes of the healer are a key factor in the control and direction of the healing energy. The healer is, apparently, a channel for receiving and transmitting healing energy which can ultimately be linked with God."

During the course of the healing symposium an energy field seemed to build up in the auditorium. After the conclusion of the last scheduled talk, hundreds of the attendees stood in line for half an hour or more for the privilege of shaking Olga Worrall's hand.

12

How Are Prayers Answered?

Although the scientific experiments reported in these pages clearly confirm the existence of a healing energy in life and the efficacy of prayer, they do not purport to prove how our prayers are answered. Nonetheless, it is certainly feasible to draw educated inferences from the evidence that has been compiled.

As we analyze this evidence, it becomes apparent that answers to prayer and requests for healing occur, not by one, but by a number of means.

The first method is contact by a patient with a source of healing energy. The scientific evidence presented here demonstrates that certain individuals generate, or are a channel for, an energy which may be transmitted by direct contact. This is the type of healing which occurred when Jesus healed the woman in the synagogue or when the woman who had been hemorraging touched the hem of His garment.

A second method is by mentally creating a condition whereby the energy which is present everywhere flows into the object or subject under treatment. The plant and cloud chamber experiments with the Worralls, and the remote healing study offer convincing evidence that healing conditions can be created from a distance.

Ambrose Worrall told of an extraordinary healing which occurred halfway around the world. He was at a meeting at Wainwright House in Rye, New York, and was telling a distinguished group of scientists, doctors, and ministers about some of his experiences with healing. One of the members of the group had a relative who was severely ill in a hospital in Karachi, Pakistan, and asked if the group would say a special prayer for her.

Ambrose described the girl to the group. "She is nineteen years old, has blue eyes, blonde hair, and weighs about 120 pounds. Let us all see her well and smiling and with healing energy just pouring into her." Each member of the group then created this mental picture in his mind and held it for about five minutes.

Two days later, the man who had asked for the prayer received a telegram from Karachi saying that two days before, at the time the group had been praying in New York, the girl had taken a remarkable turn for the better and had now been discharged from the hospital!

A third avenue of healing lies in the power of suggestion. Psychologists have demonstrated the fact that the conscious and subconscious minds operate in two completely different manners. The conscious mind is analytical, questioning, reasoning, doubting. The subconscious mind readily accepts any idea or command that is introduced and then carries out the command to the best of its ability. Once a thought is firmly implanted in the subconscious mind it can bring about corresponding changes in the body. The changes can occur gradually or, in some cases, instantaneously.

If a doctor tells a patient, "You will feel better tomorrow," and if the patient really accepts the idea, he will certainly feel better the next day. When Elisha told the leper he would be healed if he bathed in the River Jordan seven times, he may have firmly implanted the idea in the leper's subconscious mind and, when the leper followed Elisha's instructions, the healing took place.

A fourth healing mechanism, and probably the most important of all, is attunement to the source of all power and healing energy. This is done by prayer and meditation.

Prayer does not persuade an all-powerful Deity to suspend the laws of the universe for the benefit of the person who is praying. It is a method of raising the vibrations of the petitioner and bringing him to a state which enables him to receive the healing energy which is available to all.

Meditation is an even more powerful form of attunement. It allows the individual to identify with the divine life energies of the universe and focus them into his or her own consciousness—for healing, building, creating, and understanding.

These are four basic means by which prayers for healing may be answered. There are others, which are even more difficult to substantiate in the laboratory. However, if we know that some prayers are answered by an orderly and logical process, it is reasonable to assume that undeviating laws and principles govern the answers to all prayers. Our task is to discover these laws so we can apply the knowledge to make our prayers more effective.

We have been deep in the scientific forest and have had a close look at some of the trees. Let us back off and try to sketch out a picture of the total scene. When I spoke at a church retreat several years ago, I asked members of the audience for their definition of God. Some of the replies were: "God is Eternal Spirit," "God is Love," "God is the Spirit of Infinite Life." The broadest definition, one which included all the others, was "God is the total sum of the universe and its associated energies."

If God is the total of everything that exists, then, being a part of that total, each of us is a part of God. Being a part of God, we each have, if we but realize it, all the creative powers of God. If we take a drop of water from the ocean, each drop has the identical properties of any other drop. The drop differs from the ocean only in size but the qualities are the same.

This means that if we pray in accordance and in harmony with God's universal laws, we are performing a creative act and, inevitably, what we pray for will come to pass. This also means that the only limitation on what we can accomplish is our limited conception of our abilities and powers.

So it all boils down to the fact that we are all creators and are constantly creating good or bad things through the use or misuse of our power. We create by our thoughts and every thought is a prayer. Effective prayer consists of clearly imaging or imagining the situation we want to bring about. If we visualize it, believe it will come about, and do everything in our power to make it happen, the situation we pray for will manifest itself in our physical life.

13

The "Internet" of Prayer

The experiments described in this book—from accelerating the growth of rye grass to stirring up the mist in a cloud chamber six hundred miles away—verify what religious people have believed for millenia—that life energy can be harnessed by prayer and used to heal.

This energy may be emitted from the hands of healers in some instances and from their minds in other cases. It may well be a property that all humans possess to some degree, but it is clearly most pronounced in certain individuals, such as the Worralls. This energy, called "biomagnetic energy" and "paraelectricity" by modern investigators, is the life force of the ancient Chinese, the *prana* of Hindu yogis, and the odic force of Reichenbach.

The results of the distant rye grass experiment and the remote cloud chamber tests demonstrated the ability of someone like Olga Worrall to influence biological and physical systems from a distance. While the mechanism of remote mental healing is still unclear, the cloud chamber experiment with Dr. Worrall indicates that she was able to project her consciousness and energy body from Baltimore, Maryland, to the physics laboratory at Agnes Scott College in Atlanta, Georgia, where the cloud chamber was located.

If rye grass can be influenced by thought from a distance of six hundred miles, cannot the cells of our body be influenced by what we are thinking? If we wake up in the morning and say, "I surely feel lousy today," do our cells hear us and make our words come true?

If, instead of grumbling, you would say, "I feel fine!" ten times—and really believe it—are you not apt to feel better? These experiments suggest that you are.

The experiments with remote mental healing also suggest that Carl Jung's "collective unconscious" actually exists and is common to all living creatures. With such a thought and energy link connecting us all, it would not be necessary for a healer to transmit energy to distant sites. Instead, by contacting the collective unconscious, through his subconscious mind, a healer could influence the subconscious of a patient so that he could more readily absorb energy already present in his environment.

To put it in other words, each of us is like a computer terminal. By accessing the central computer memory bank, we can influence or instruct any other terminal hooked into the system. This is actually the way the Internet or World Wide Web systems operate.

When the Worralls would pray for people all over the world, they would instruct their patients to get completely relaxed and to think of them at exactly 9:00 p.m. in the evening. Many patients who followed these instructions were healed or significantly improved.

Cleve Baxter's experiment in which a philodendron plant reacted violently to the death of brine shrimp demonstrated that there is a link between all living systems. The results of his work indicate that we live in an energy field and our thoughts influence other living systems around us. I was able to verify this in experiments I conducted with Olga Worrall and a philodendron plant of our own.

Using the same type of brain wave monitor used by Cleve Baxter, I connected the electrodes to a leaf on the plant and had Olga mentally transmit different types of thoughts to the plant. When she visualized the plant as being robust and excited, the frequency and the amplitude of the trace on the strip chart recorder increased. Simply talking about the plant produced a small reaction, but when Dr. Worrall projected her consciousness into the plant the needle went almost off scale. When Olga visualized the plant as being filled with God's healing energies, the plant responded dramatically. After the healing treatment, the plant's recording returned to its normal low frequency, low amplitude base line.

During these experiments, Olga's brain wave frequency always dropped to the alpha state (eight cycles per second) or lower in a matter of seconds before she began her mental healing treatments. Most individuals require about twenty minutes to achieve this degree of relaxation.

At one point during these experiments, Olga was in the laboratory and we were establishing a good base line trace for the philodendron plant. Then Dr. Joseph Cornish, a friend of Olga's whom she had not seen for several years, entered the room and greeted her very warmly, giving her a big hug and a kiss.

When we examined the trace on the strip chart recorder we discovered that the plant had dramatic reactions to these goings on. When Dr. Cornish first entered the room, the amplitude rose slightly. When they embraced, the strip chart pen went completely off the scale!

Love is a flow of energy and the philodendron plant was reacting to that energy. Indeed, many authorities contend that love is the central essence of the energies that heal. This episode would tend to confirm this supposition.

We know that orphans are not as healthy and do not grow as rapidly as do children with loving parents. Why? Because they are deprived of a major source of energy.

The existence of the atom bomb, which is a direct result of the mathematical theories of Einstein, is proof that energy and matter are interchangeable. Scientific experiments have demonstrated that some people are capable of bending metal objects enclosed in sealed glass cylinders by concentrating their thoughts on them. Thus it has been established that matter can be controlled and directed by thought, and that thought is a form of energy.

The experiments described in this book were all conducted using standard scientific methods and tests. The results are consistent with what science knows today about life in this universe. Not only have these experiments proved that prayer is effective, but they have also demonstrated that God and science can both be found in the laboratory. In its highest calling, science reveals to us the ways and laws of God, even as God calls us to use our science wisely and intelligently.

Why is someone like Olga or Ambrose Worrall an outstanding healer, while most of the rest of us are not? It may be nothing more complicated than the simple fact that Ambrose and Olga had learned how to pray effectively.

It is to be hoped that this book will help inspire others to learn to pray effectively as well.

14

Epilogue

After the conclusion of these experiments, we remained close friends with Ambrose and Olga. They continued to give our twins, Bobbie and Kristie, healing treatments at periodic intervals. Both children progressed, mentally and physically, far beyond the expectations of the psychologists and doctors who treated them in their early years. They learned to read first and second grade books and were able to write simple sentences.

With the help of private tutoring, Kristie was able to do simple algebra problems. Bobbie developed fine motor skills and learned to do exquisite embroidery.

Unfortunately, at the age of fifteen, Kristie developed a problem with lupus and, despite all the doctors could do, progressively weakened, until she passed away.

We thought we had located an ideal environment for Bobbie at Annandale Village at Suwanee,

Georgia. Annandale Village was founded by Dr. and Mrs. Maxwell Berry, who had a retarded child of their own. They traveled all over Europe visiting schools and homes for handicapped adults. They combined the best features of all in their design for Annandale. In a 30-acre rural environment, they built attractive dormitories and facilities to provide maximum comfort and educational opportunities for the villagers. Each handicapped adult had a specially designed program. Many learned to perform useful tasks and worked at nearby stores and restaurants during the daytime.

Bobbie was getting along quite well when disaster struck. One night, one of the inmates started a fire in her dormitory and Bobbie and seven of her companions perished of smoke inhalation.

Ambrose Worrall died of a heart attack at the age of 73 in February, 1972. Olga continued her work at the New Life Clinic at Mt. Washington Methodist Church in Baltimore. She frequently addressed nurses and doctors at medical schools. She gave talks on healing and prayer all over the United States and Europe and, on one occasion, lectured in Japan.

Olga left this plane of existence about fifteen years after her husband died. Her philosophy, as it relates to the subject of this book, is expressed in the following statement she made to her parishioners at the New Life Clinic:

"I have no bag of tricks—no mumbo jumbo. Faith healing is a technique that goes back to Biblical times, and we have plenty of evidence that it works. Most religions still believe in it, but few still practice it—which is a pity. Anything that permitted miracles to be performed 2,000 years ago is still in existence, if only we would make use of it. "

It is hoped that the ideas presented in this book will encourage others to solve their problems by creating their own "miracles in the making"—through effective prayer.

References

1. Grad, B., Cadoret, R., and Paul, G.I., *International Journal of Parapsychology*, Vol. III, No. 2 (1961).
2. Smith, J.,"Approaches to Healing: Laying on of Hands," *Human Dimensions*, Vol. 1 & 2, Buffalo, N.Y., 1976.
3. Glasser,O., and Barth, H., *Radiology, 30*, 62-67, January 1938.
4. Carlova, J., *Medical Economics*, 99-114, September 17, 1973.
5. Reichenbach, K. von, *Letters on Od and Magnetism*. University Books, London, 1968.
6. Eden, J., *Animal Magnetism*, Exposition Press, Hicksville, N.Y., 1974.
7. Ostrander, S., and Schroeder, L., *Psychic Discoveries Behind the Iron Curtain*, Prentice-Hall, Inc., 1970.
8. De La Warr, G.W., and Baker, D., *Biomagnetism*, 53-56, De La Warr Laboratories, Oxford, 1967.
9. Schmidt, A.X., and Marlies, C.A., *Principles of High Polymer Theory and Practice*, 33-34, McGraw-Hill, New York, N.Y., 1946.
10. Worrall, A. and Worrall, O., *Explore Your Psychic World*, Ariel Press, Columbus & Atlanta, 1989.
11. Yogananda, P., *Autobiography of a Yogi*, 415-490, Self-Realization Fellowship, Los Angeles, 1955.
12. Reich, W., "Discovery of the Orgone," *International Journal of Sex Economy and Orgone Research*, Vol. 1, 1942.
13. Galton, F., *Inquiries into Human Faculty and its Development*, pp. 277-294, MacMillan, London, 1863.
14. Carrel, A., *Man the Unknown*, pp. 148-149, Harper & Row, New York, 1934.
15. Joyce. C.R.B., and Weldon, R.M.C., "The Objective Efficacy of Prayer," *J. Chron. Dis.*, 1965, Vol. 18, pp. 367-377.
16. Snedecor, W. and Cochran, W.G., *Statistical Methods*, University of Iowa Press, Ames, Iowa, 1977.

About the Author

Dr. Robert N. Miller received his B.S., M.S. and Ph.D. degrees in chemical engineering from The Ohio State University. While at Ohio State, he was a varsity center and linebacker on a Big Ten championship football team. In 1941, he married music major Genevieve Alberta Kohler.

Miller was a professor of chemical engineering at the Georgia Institute of Technology for fifteen years, serving also as an assistant football coach. In his three years as varsity line coach, the Yellow Jackets played in the Cotton Bowl, Sugar Bowl, and the Orange Bowl.

In 1956, Bob joined Lockheed Aeronautical Systems Co. of Marietta, Georgia, as a staff scientist. At Lockheed, he was responsible for Air Force and Navy programs relating to electrochemistry, radioisotopes, surface chemistry, protective coatings, and corrosion. He was responsible for the development of a corrosion inhibiting sealant and primer that is used worldwide. He also developed a coating system with a crack growth inhibitor that extends the service life of aircraft. In 1986 he received the Frank Speller International Award for Outstanding Contributions to Corrosion Engineering.

Dr. Miller's most recent invention is the Lockheed Smog Eliminator, a device which reduces contaminants in automobile exhaust emissions and also gives a five percent increase in gasoline mileage. Lockheed has obtained a patent and will produce the device, distributing it to the automotive industry.

Dr. Miller is a member of Mensa and Tau Beta Pi, has presented or published more than sixty scientific papers, is holder of fourteen U. S. patents, and is listed in *American Men of Science* and *Who's Who in the South and Southeast.*

Suggested Reading

For those who wish to learn more about effective prayer, healing, and meditation, as well as about Ambrose and Olga Worrall, the following books are recommended:

The Gift of Healing, by Ambrose and Olga Worrall.

Explore Your Psychic World, by Ambrose and Olga Worrall.

The Way To Health, by Robert R. Leichtman, M.D. and Carl Japikse.

Making Prayer Work, by Robert R. Leichtman, M.D. and Carl Japikse.

Active Meditation, by Robert R. Leichtman, M.D. and Carl Japikse.

All of these books are published by Ariel Press, 289 S. Main Street, #205, Alpharetta, GA 30201. They may be ordered by telephone by calling 1-800-336-7769. Books by Ernest Holmes about the Science of Mind can also be ordered through Ariel Press.